Discovering Biblical Treasures

Understanding 1 Thessalonians

Using Ancient Bible Study Methods with a new foundation

Michael Harvey Koplitz

Acknowledgments

This work could not have been accomplished without Dr. Anne Davis, who taught me Ancient Bible (Hebraic) study methods, and my two study partners, Rev. Dr. Robert Cook and Pastor Sandra Koplitz. We know that the journey has just started and will last a lifetime. The discovery of the depths of God's Word is waiting for us to find.

Table of Contents

Introduction

When a person is baptized as an infant and grows up in the church, different paradigms become a part of their religious DNA. The church has a message to give about Jesus Christ and His importance. Very few people study the theology and doctrines of the church to determine for themselves the accuracy of the church. The Proto-Orthodox church, which survived the pressures of the Roman Empire, decided in its infancy to oppose any expression of Christianity that did not fit its dogma. In addition, the Proto-Orthodox church would permanently destroy any writings that the rival Christians had developed.

The Gnostic Christians of Northern Egypt viewed the life of Jesus of Nazareth in a completely different way than the Proto-Orthodox church did. They saw the message about the Kingdom of Heaven as the vital purpose of Jesus. His birth, death, and Resurrection are not mentioned in the Gnostic Gospels. However, did the Proto-Orthodox church destroy the Gnostic Gospels when they crushed said movement? The answer is yes and no. Yes, they destroyed what they got their hands on. No, because in 1948, copies of the Gnostic religious books were discovered in Alexandria, Egypt. Once these documents were translated, the world learned what the Gnostic Christians believed. It is fascinatingly different than what the Proto-Orthodox said about these followers of Christ.

Why is this understanding critical? Much research points to a different situation in the early years than what the church espouses. A lot of this information is available to anyone today. However, the Seminaries and churches will not openly talk about these other writings about Jesus and His disciples. The scholars teaching in most Seminaries have learned their lessons from the church and from closed-minded mentors who refuse to look at other possibilities. This is because the Western European world took Christianity and changed it from a Near Eastern religion to a Western religion.

There is a theory that Paul converted Mithras House Churches into Jesus House Churches. This is clear from the connection between the Mithras' and Christianity's rituals. For example, baptism was the initiation ritual of Mithras. Communion did not originate with Jesus. This ritual was a part of Mithras where the followers would share his flesh (bread) and drink his blood (wine). There are many more rituals that Christianity picked up from Mithras. A good reference is "Christianity's Need for Mithras," which the author wrote.

Did Paul create the churches in the letters he sent, which comprise the New Testament, and if so, they must have been Jewish groups who became Jewish-Christians? They would have continued with their Hebraic rituals and saw Jesus of Nazareth as the Messiah that the prophets of old had promised. They would have adopted as many as Jesus' teachings and tried to live by them. The letters in the New Testament are written in Greek. However, most Jews in the Roman Empire did not speak Greek; instead, they spoke Aramaic and Hebrew. These congregations would not have understood a Greek letter from Paul.

Therefore, the letters in the New Testament must have been written in Aramaic and then transliterated into Greek. The same can be said for the Gospels, all of them. The church, over the centuries, decided who wrote the Gospels and what their intent was. The only Gospel we can assign to a writer is Luke. The other three are up in the air about who actually wrote them. While in Seminary, the author was taught that the entire New Testament was originally written in Koine Greek. However, that raised the question of, "Did Jesus speak Greek?" The Seminary instructors said, "no, Jesus did not speak Greek." Then the New Testament, especially the Gospels, must have been written in Aramaic. After all, Jesus spoke Aramaic and Hebrew.

We know this because He was a poor *tekton* (a stonemason or carpenter) from an impoverished city named Nazareth. Being born to a Jewish family in Galilee, he would have learned the traditions of His people and trade. He would have learned to speak Aramaic, the language of the area. He would have learned Hebrew because that was the language of the synagogue and the Temple in Jerusalem. In other words, Hebrew was the language of God, and Jewish males learned the language.

Suppose you are ready to toss this manuscript into the nearest trash can or delete it off your electronic device at this point in the introduction. In that case, the writer has your attention. This is the reaction when the writer has spoken with persons who had been indoctrinated into the church's position since birth. The author did not come into the church environment until he was 35. Therefore, the church's paradigms, dogma, and doctrine were not a part of his DNA. Instead, he questioned a lot. He found many inconsistencies between the Bible and the doctrines of the church. Seminary was an experience to learn what the church had evolved into two-thousand years after the death of Jesus.

There are more parts to the overall premise that the New Testament was originally written in Aramaic and will be explored. For the reader to grasp the subsequent phases of the proof, an open mind is critical.

Culture and Language

Let us continue in the journey of examining the New Testament to determine its original language. Nothing in stone tells us that Aramaic is the Original Language of the New Testament. However, nothing says that Koine Greek was the original language of the New Testament either. Therefore, we have two theories about the original language of the New Testament. The author admits that the Seminary he attended drove home the belief that the Old Testament was written in Hebrew, except for a few spots. The New Testament was initially written in Koine Greek.

The writers' research has been searching for the original meaning of Scripture for many years. The methodology for this work is called "Ancient Bible Study Methods." The method was developed by Dr. Anne Davis of the Bible Learning University in Albuquerque, New Mexico. The author studied this method with Dr. Davis as his mentor. It became clear that the search for the original meaning of the Scriptures requires that the culture and language be examined. So, the author's methodology is Dr. Davis' work, plus his Ph.D. studies combining the method, culture, and language.

The language examination is easy for the Old Testament because it was written in Hebrew, and about one-half of Daniel is in Aramaic. It does not take long to realize that idioms and figures of speech in the Hebrew of the Old Testament revealed a lot about the people and situation of the day when the scrolls were written. The Targums were a valuable resource because they are the Aramaic translations the rabbis did for the people living outside of Judea. The rabbis added commentary to the Targums because they knew that some of the idioms and speech used in the Near East would not translate well into the different areas where the Jews lived.

The culture of the Near East has been essentially the same in many aspects since the days of Jesus. Many practices of Jesus' day are still in use today. The culture of the Jews of the Near East is built into the language. Many times an Aramaic or Hebrew word has a deep meaning that is only fully understood by natives who are living in that culture. The Old Testament is filled with cultural items that do not need to be spelled out because the people knew their culture at the author's time.

Suppose the New Testament in Koine Greek is a transliteration of the Aramaic. The culture, figures of speech, and idioms will be easy to identify when examining the Peshitta (the Aramaic version of the New Testament). Indeed many of the so-called difficult words of Jesus are not tricky when examined in the light of the culture of Jesus' day. An example is, "faith to move a mountain," Jesus said these words to His disciples. The church determined that this meant a complete faith in Jesus. From the western European Greek point of view, that makes sense. What else could it possibly mean?

"Faith to move a mountain" is an Aramaic idiomatic expression. What Jesus said to His followers when he said this is that his disciples needed to be faithful so that they could change the "government's view through their words." The governing body for Judaism resided on the top of a mountain. Jerusalem, with its Temple, was built on the top of Mount Zion, a very tall mountain. This idiom survived because the Aramaic Gospels were transliterated into Koine Greek. Numerous other examples support this position.

Suppose the culture and language idioms of Jesus' day can be found in the Koine Greek because it was transliterated. In that case, it supports the theory of the Aramaic versions being the original language of the Gospels and possibly even more.

The Aramaic Version of the New Testament

The Peshitta is the accepted Aramaic translation of the New Testament for many churches of the East. Peshitta means "simple, true, direct, and original." It is a collection of scrolls that were compiled in 150 CE. There were some revisions to the Peshitta in the fifth and sixth centuries. The Greek version of the New Testament is a transliteration of the Peshitta.[1]

For centuries, the Catholic church has been using the Latin version of the Bible, the Vulgate, and still uses it. The Vulgate was developed around 350 CE by Jerome by order of the Pope at that time. Erasmus (1466 – 1536) was the person who put together the Greek New Testament for the Catholic church.

"The New Testament, brought to light in the original Greek tongue, was compiled and made available for humanity to study and learn. Although working under and deeply associated with the Roman Catholic Church, the learned scholar declared his disagreement with those who wanted to keep the Scriptures from the common people. He said, "If only the farmer would sing something from them at his plow, the weaver moves his shuttle to their tune, the traveler lighten the boredom of his journey with Scriptural stories!" Little did he know, the work he was about to produce would change the world forever. This Greek New Testament, in printed form, would become the standard of the New Testament, launching the translations of Martin Luther and William Tyndale into the world. Thus, fulfilling his dream that all men would read the

---

[1] Rocco A. Errico and George M. Lamsa, *Aramaic Light on Galatians through Hebrews: A Commentary Based on Aramaic, the Language of Jesus, and Ancient near Eastern Customs* (Smyrna, GA: Noohra Foundation, 2005).

Bible for themselves in their common language. His new "study Bible" had two main parts, the Greek text, and a revised Latin edition, which was more elegant and accurate than the traditional translation of Jerome's Latin Vulgate. Erasmus prefaced this monumental work of scholarship with an exhortation to Bible study. He proclaimed that the New Testament contains the "philosophy of Christ," simple and accessible teaching with the power to transform lives."[2]

The church recognized Erasmus' Greek New Testament in 1515 CE. The church in the Near East has been using the Peshitta as the original language of the New Testament since 150 CE. If the Greek New Testament was important to the church as an original language, then why did it adopt the Vulgate in 350 CE? The church should have adopted the Greek New Testament at the beginning.

The Peshitta, translated into English, is used to examine Paul's letters. The rest of the methodology that the author developed for Ancient Bible Study Methods is the framework of this research.

---

[2] "Erasmus Greek New Testament," Insight of the King, accessed February 18, 2022, https://www.insightoftheking.com/erasmus-greek-new-testament.html.

The Messianic Tradition Change

One problem for Peter and the Disciples was that they claimed Yeshua to be the Messiah that the prophets of the Hebrew Scriptures spoke of. However, Yeshua did not do what these traditions said. The main tradition was that the Messiah would destroy oppressive Romans and reinstate the Kingdom of Israel. Yeshua would then be declared the king and sit on David's throne in Jerusalem. That did not occur.

None of the messianic traditions of the day worked. So, what was the new movement going to do? They turned to the prophets and discovered Isaiah 50-53. These chapters are referred to as the Suffering Servant chapters. The Yeshua movement decided that the Suffering Servant was Yeshua. The portrayal of Yeshua's life does fit the Suffering Servant chapters. However, rabbinical interpretation then and now sees the Suffering Servant as the nation of Israel. Indeed, these chapters do describe the history of Israel. Nations have wanted to destroy the Jewish people since the time of Abraham.

The diaspora from the Babylonia Exile and the Assyrian invasions looked to squelch the Jewish people. The LORD promised that a remnant of the people would always survive. That is true throughout the 4,000-year history of the Jewish people. Many nations tried to destroy them, and the LORD intervened to ensure that a remnant of the people survived.

Paul must have been convinced in his encounter with Yeshua on the Damascus road that Yeshua was the Suffering Servant. It is clear from Paul's writings that he did believe this. For Paul, the Messiah was the Spiritual Messiah that the Kabbalah spoke. The

Kabbalah says that there will be two Messiahs. This is based on Zachariah 9:9. The first Messiah is Messiah ben Joseph. This Messiah was to restore the Kingdom of Heaven, which is a spiritual Kingdom. The second Messiah will be Messiah ben David. This Messiah was to restore the Kingdom of Israel. The Midrash from the Kabbalah did not state that the Messiah was two different souls.

The Kabbalah

There is a large amount of material in print about the Kabbalah. The Kabbalah referred to is Moses's Secret Work from Mount Sinai. Legends say Moses received three items on Mount Sinai when he met the LORD. The first is the written Law. The written Law is called the Torah. The second is the oral law. The oral law was put into a written form around 200 CE called the Mishnah. The third is the secret law called the Kabbalah. The secrets of the Kabbalah are based on the Torah and were written down around 200 CE. The main books of the Kabbalah are the Zohar and the Book of Creation.

Many of Yeshua's statements have Kabbalah undertones. Yeshua would have known the Kabbalah. Paul would have known the basics, at least, of the Kabbalah because of his religious education and training.

There are Kabbalistic ideas in the Gospels and Paul's letters. Kabbalistic verses will be highlighted in the chapters of the letters.

Methodology

The methodology employed is to use "Ancient Bible Study Methods" integrated with Jesus's day's customs and culture to examine the Hebrew and Christian Scriptures, thus gathering a more in-depth understanding by learning the Scriptures in the way the people of Jesus's day did.

I have titled the methodology of analyzing a passage of Scripture in a Hebraic manner the "Process of Discovery." The author developed this methodology, which brings together various linguistic and cultural understanding areas. There are several sections to the process, and not all the parts apply to every passage of Scripture. The overall result of developing this process is to give the reader a framework for studying the Word in more depth.

The "Process of Discovery" starts with a Scripture passage. An examination of the linguistic structure of the passage is next. The linguistic structure includes parallelism, chiastic structures, and repetition. Formatting the passage in its linguistic form allows the reader to visualize what the first century C.E. listener was hearing. Their corresponding sections label the chiasms, for example, A, B, C, B', A.' Not all passages of the Scriptures have a poetic form.

The next step is to "question the narrative." The narrative process of questioning the narrative assumes the reader knows nothing about the passage. Therefore, the questions go from the simple to the complex. The next task is to identify any linguistic patterns. Linguistic patterns include, but are not limited to, irony, simile, metaphor, symbolism, idioms, hyperbole, figurative language, personification, and allegory.

A review of any translation inconsistencies discovered between the English NAU version and either the Hebrew or Greek versions is done. There are times when a Hebrew or Greek word is translated in more than one way. Inconsistencies also can be created by the translation committee, which may have decided to use traditional language instead of the actual translation. The decision of the translation committee is in the Preface or Introduction to the Bible. Perhaps some of the inconsistencies were intentionally added to convey some deeper meaning. An examination for every discrepancy is done.

The passage is analyzed for any echoes of the Hebrew Scriptures in the Christian Scriptures. An echo occurs using a passage from the Hebrew Scriptures in the Christian Scriptures.[3] Also, echoes are found when Torah (Genesis through Deuteronomy) passages are used in other Hebrew Bible books. Cross-references in the Scripture are references from one verse to another verse, which can help the reader understand the verse.

The names of persons mentioned in the passage are listed. Many of the Hebrew names have meaning and may be associated with places or actions. Jewish parents used to name their children based on what they felt God had in store for their child. An example of this is Abraham, whose original name was Abram and was changed to mean eternal father (God changed Abram's name to Abraham, indicating a function he was to perform). When the Hebrew Bible gives names, many occurrences mean something unique. The same importance can occur for the names of places. The time it takes to travel between locations can supply insight into the event.

---

[3] Mitzvot are the 613 commandments found in the Torah that please God. There are positive and negative commandments. The list was first development by Maimonides. The full list can be found at: ttp://www.jewfaq.org/613.htm.

Keyphrases are identified in verses when they are essential to understanding that passage. There are no rules for selecting the keywords. Searching for other occurrences of the keywords in Scripture in a concordance is necessary to understand the Word's usage; this must be done in either Hebrew or Greek, not in English. A classic Hebraic approach is to find the usage of a word in the Scripture by finding other verses that contain the Word. The usage of a word in its original language is discovered by searching the Scripture in the language of the Word. Verses that contain the Word are identified, and a pattern for the usage of the Word is discovered. Each verse is examined to see what the usage of the Word is, which may reveal a model for the Word's usage. The first usage of the Word in the Scripture, primarily if used in the Torah, is essential for Hebrew words. For the Greek words, the Christian Scriptures are used to determine the Word usage in the Scripture. Sometimes, it can be very helpful to find the equivalent Greek Word in the Septuagint and then analyze its Hebrew usage.

The Rules of Hillel are used when applicable. Hillel was a Torah scholar who lived shortly before Jesus's day. Hillel developed several rules for Torah students to interpret the Scriptures, which refer to halachic Midrash. In several cases, these rules are helpful in the analysis of the Scripture.

The cultural implications from the writing period are done after the linguistic analysis is completed. The culture is crucial because it is not explicitly referenced in the biblical narratives, as indicated earlier.

From the linguistic analysis and the cultural understanding, it is possible to obtain a deeper meaning of the Scripture beyond the plain text's literal meaning. That is what the listeners of Jesus's time were doing. They put linguistics and culture together without even having to contemplate it.

The analysis will lead to a set of findings explaining what the passage meant in Jesus's day. Most of the time, the Hebraic analysis leads to the desire for more in-depth analysis to fully understand what Jesus was talking about or what was happening to Him. Whatever the result, a new, more in-depth understanding of the Scripture is obtained.

The components of the Process of Discovery are:

Language

Process of Discovery

Linguistics Section

Linguistic Structure

Discussion

Questioning the Passage

Verse Comparison of citations or proof text

Translation Inconsistencies

Biblical Personalities

Biblical Locations

Phrase Study

Linguistic Echoes

Rules of Hillel

Culture Section

Discussion

Questioning the passage

Cultural Echoes

Culture and Linguistics Section

Discussion

Thoughts

Reflections

Only the applicable sections are included in this document.

Introduction to the Letter

Most New Testament scholars believe that this is the oldest letter Paul wrote. It was probably penned around 50 C.E. Thessalonica was a city comprised mainly of Jews who had left Judea to find a new home. There were Mithras house churches in the city along with the synagogues.

In this letter, Paul admonishes the congregation to stay loyal to Yeshua's teachings and refrain from sexual immorality. Paul also talked about the return of Yeshua.[4]

---

[4] Rocco A. Errico and George M. Lamsa, *Aramaic Light on Galatians through Hebrews: A Commentary Based on Aramaic, the Language of Jesus, and Ancient near Eastern Customs* (Smyma, GA: Noohra Foundation, 2005).

Chapter One

Language

Peshitta in English	New American Standard 1995
1 Th. 1:1 I Paul and Sylvanus and Timothy, to the church of the Thessalonians, which is in God the Father and in our Lord Jesus the Messiah: Grace be with you, and peace. 2 We give thanks to God at all times, on account of you all, and remember you continually in our prayers: 3 and we call to mind before God the Father the works of your faith, and the toil of your love, and the patience of your hope in our Lord Jesus the Messiah. 4 For we know your election, my brethren, beloved of God. 5 For our preaching among you, was not in words only; but also in power, and in the Holy Spirit, and in genuine persuasion. Ye also know, how we were among you for your sakes. 6 And ye became imitators of us, and of our Lord, in that ye received the word in great affliction, and with the joy of the Holy Spirit. 7 And ye were a pattern for all the believers who are in Macedonia and in Achaia. 8 For from you the word of our Lord sounded forth; [and] not only in Macedonia and Achaia, but in every place, your faith in God is heard of; so that we have no need to say any thing concerning you. 9 For they declare, what an ingress we had to you, and how ye turned from the worship of idols unto God, that ye might worship the living and true God; 10 while ye wait for his Son from heaven, that Jesus whom he raised from the dead, who delivereth us from the wrath to come.	1Th. 1:1 *a*Paul and *b*Silvanus and *c*Timothy, To the *d*church of the Thessalonians in God the Father and the Lord Jesus Christ: *e*Grace to you and peace. 1Th. 1:2 *a*We give thanks to God always for all of you, *b*making mention *of you* in our prayers; 3 constantly bearing in mind your *a*work of faith and labor of *b*love and 1*c*steadfastness of hope 2in our Lord Jesus Christ in the presence of *d*our God and Father, 4 knowing, *a*brethren beloved by God, *b*His choice of you; 5 for our *a*gospel did not come to you in word only, but also *b*in power and in the Holy Spirit and with *c*full conviction; just as you know *d*what kind of men we 1proved to be among you for your sake. 6 You also became *a*imitators of us and of the Lord, *b*having received *c*the word in much tribulation with the *d*joy of the Holy Spirit, 7 so that you became an example to all the believers in *a*Macedonia and in *b*Achaia. 8 For *a*the word of the Lord has *b*sounded forth from you, not only in *c*Macedonia and *d*Achaia, but also *e*in every place your faith toward God has gone forth, so that we have no need to say anything. 9 For they themselves report about us what kind of a 1*a*reception we had 2with you, and how you *b*turned to God *c*from 3idols to serve 4*d*a living and true God, 10 and to *a*wait for His Son from 1heaven, whom

	He [b]raised from the dead, *that is* Jesus, who [c]rescues us from [d]the wrath to come.

References to the New American Standard 1995

1Thessalonians 1:1
[a]2 Thess 1:1
[b]2 Cor 1:19
[c]Acts 16:1
[d]Acts 17:1
[e]Rom 1:7

1Thessalonians 1:2
[a]Rom 1:8; 2 Thess 1:3
[b]Rom 1:9

1Thessalonians 1:3
[1]Or *perseverance*
[2]Lit *of*
[a]John 6:29
[b]1 Cor 13:13
[c]Rom 8:25; 15:4
[d]Gal 1:4

1Thessalonians 1:4
[a]Rom 1:7; 2 Thess 2:13
[b]2 Pet 1:10

1Thessalonians 1:5
[1]Or *became*
[a]1 Cor 9:14
[b]Rom 15:19
[c]Luke 1:1; Col 2:2
[d]1 Thess 2:10

1Thessalonians 1:6
[a]1 Cor 4:16; 11:1f
[b]Acts 17:5-10
[c]2 Tim 4:2
[d]Acts 13:52; 2 Cor 6:10; Gal 5:22

1Thessalonians 1:7
[a]Rom 15:26
[b]Acts 18:12

1Thessalonians 1:8
[a]Col 3:16; 2 Thess 3:1
[b]Rom 10:18
[c]Rom 15:26
[d]Acts 18:12
[e]Rom 1:8; 16:19; 2 Cor 2:14

1Thessalonians 1:9
[1]Lit *entrance*
[2]Lit *to*
[3]Or *the idols*
[4]Or *the*
[a]1 Thess 2:1
[b]Acts 14:15
[c]1 Cor 12:2
[d]Matt 16:16

1Thessalonians 1:10
[1]Lit *the heavens*
[a]Matt 16:27f; 1 Cor 1:7
[b]Acts 2:24
[c]Rom 5:9
[d]Matt 3:7; 1 Thess 2:16; 5:9

Koine Greek

1Th. 1:1   Παυλος και Σιλουανος και Τιμοθεος, τη εκκλησια Θεσσαλονικεων εν θεω πατρι, και κυριω Ιησου χριστω· χαρις υμιν και ειρηνη απο θεου πατρος ημων και κυριου Ιησου χριστου.

1Th. 1:2   Ευχαριστουμεν τω θεω παντοτε περι παντων υμων, μνειαν υμων ποιουμενοι επι των προσευχων ημων, ³ αδιαλειπτως μνημονευοντες υμων του εργου της πιστεως, και του κοπου της αγαπης, και της υπομονης της ελπιδος του κυριου ημων Ιησου χριστου, εμπροσθεν του θεου και πατρος ημων· ⁴ ειδοτες, αδελφοι ηγαπημενοι υπο θεου, την εκλογην υμων· ⁵ οτι το ευαγγελιον ημων ουκ εγενηθη εις υμας εν λογω μονον, αλλα και εν δυναμει, και εν πνευματι αγιω, και εν πληροφορια πολλη, καθως οιδατε οιοι εγενηθημεν εν υμιν δι' υμας. ⁶ Και υμεις μιμηται ημων εγενηθητε και του κυριου, δεξαμενοι τον λογον εν θλιψει πολλη μετα χαρας πνευματος αγιου, ⁷ ωστε γενεσθαι υμας τυπους πασιν τοις πιστευουσιν εν τη Μακεδονια και τη Αχαια. ⁸ Αφ' υμων γαρ εξηχηται ο λογος του κυριου ου μονον εν τη Μακεδονια και εν τη Αχαια, αλλα και εν παντι τοπω η πιστις υμων η προς τον θεον εξεληλυθεν, ωστε μη χρειαν ημας εχειν λαλειν τι. ⁹ αυτοι γαρ περι ημων απαγγελλουσιν οποιαν εισοδον εσχομεν προς υμας, και πως επεστρεψατε προς τον θεον απο των ειδωλων, δουλευειν θεω ζωντι και αληθινω, ¹⁰ και αναμενειν τον υιον αυτου εκ των ουρανων, ον ηγειρεν εκ των νεκρων, Ιησουν, τον ρυομενον ημας απο της οργης της ερχομενης.

Process of Discovery

Linguistics Section

Linguistic Structure

1. 1Th. 1:1 I Paul and Sylvanus and Timothy, to the church of the Thessalonians, which is in God the Father and in our Lord Jesus the Messiah: Grace be with you, and peace.

    Paul does not refer to Yeshua as God. This verse indicates that this church was a mainly Jewish congregation. The idea of the Messiah coming who was not divine was acceptable to these people.

2. [3] and we call to mind before God the Father the works of your faith, and the toil of your love, and the patience of your hope in our Lord Jesus the Messiah. This verse is another example of Paul referring to Yeshua as the Messiah, not as divine.

The NASB 1995 was used for the chiastic structure.

A [1] *Paul and *Silvanus and *Timothy,
To the *church of the Thessalonians in God the Father and the Lord Jesus Christ: *Grace to you and peace. [2] *We give thanks to God always for all of you, *making mention *of you* in our prayers; [3] constantly bearing in mind your *work of faith and labor of *love and [1c]steadfastness of hope [2]in our Lord Jesus Christ in the presence of *our God and Father,

> **B** [4] knowing, *brethren beloved by God, *His* choice of you; [5] for our *gospel did not come to you in word only, but also *in power and in the Holy Spirit and with *full conviction; just as you know *what kind of men we [1]proved to be among you for your sake.

B' [6] You also became [a]imitators of us and of the Lord, [b]having received [c]the word in much tribulation with the [d]joy of the Holy Spirit, [7] so that you became an example to all the believers in [a]Macedonia and in [b]Achaia.

A' [8] For [a]the word of the Lord has [b]sounded forth from you, not only in [c]Macedonia and [d]Achaia, but also [e]in every place your faith toward God has gone forth, so that we have no need to say anything. [9] For they themselves report about us what kind of a [1a]reception we had [2]with you, and how you [b]turned to God [c]from [3]idols to serve [4d]a living and true God, [10] and to [a]wait for His Son from [1]heaven, whom He [b]raised from the dead, *that is* Jesus, who [c]rescues us from [d]the wrath to come.

A: Faith. B: Words and the Holy Spirit.[5]

Discussion

This chapter is a standard greeting. Paul praises the congregation for their faith in Yeshua and for following Yeshua's way.

Questioning the narrative

1. What does it mean to be elected? (v. 4)

   The people in this congregation are called the elect because they had abandoned their ways in order to live a life according to the teachings of Yeshua. Paul believed that anyone who came to faith in Yeshua, meaning that they followed Yeshua's way, were "elected" into the Kingdom of Heaven. Therefore, to be elected was to become a subject of the Kingdom of Heaven. The entrance was gained by following Yeshua's example and having faith in what Yeshua spoke of when he lived.

---

[5] Hajime Murai, "Literary Structure (Chiasm, Chiasmus) of First Epistle to the Thessalonians," Literary structure (chiasm, chiasmus) of each pericopes of First Epistle to the Thessalonians, accessed July 20, 2022, http://www.bible.literarystructure.info/bible/52_1Thessalonians_pericope_e.html.

2. What did Paul think the Holy Spirit was? (v. 5)

The Holy Spirit is another way of naming the Shekinah. The Shekinah is the essence of the LORD's characteristics. In the Kabbalah, the Shekinah is the Spirit of the LORD in the Sefirah Malkhut. One can feel the LORD's presence through the Shekinah. When the Hebrews traveled in the Sinai, the Shekinah guided them. Therefore, Paul is telling the congregation to continue to let the Shekinah lead them in their new lives of faith in Yeshua. Modern scholars tend to overlook that the idea of the Trinity was not formalized until Origen's day, around 180 CE. The Kabbalah view of the "Holy Spirit" is what existed in Paul's day.

3. What is verse ten referring to?

This verse is referring to the idea that Yeshua would return. The idea of Yeshua's second coming can be traced to two ideas. The Mithras cult believed that Mithras, the cult's Messiah, would someday return to collect his followers. When Paul converted Mithras House churches, the concept of the second coming in Christianity changed to the Mithras belief. Since this is a Jewish congregation, the idea of the return of Yeshua comes from the Kabbalah. Zachariah 9:9 is the basis of the Kabbalah belief. This verse refers to the Messiah coming on a colt and a donkey. The Gospels have difficulty with this verse and have Yeshua entering Jerusalem on Palm Sunday on two animals. The Kabbalah belief is that there are two Messiahs. The first Messiah is named Messiah ben Joseph. This Messiah was to restore the spiritual kingdom of the Jewish people. This is what Yeshua was trying to do. He was trying to reform the spiritual awareness and nature of Judaism. The second coming of the Messiah was Messiah ben David. This second Messiah was to bring the armed revolt that would over through all oppressors of the LORD's people and reestablish the Kingdom of David. Therefore, since the

Thessalonian congregation was Jewish they probably viewed Yeshua as Messiah ben Joseph. They would be awaiting the arrival of Messiah ben David.

Biblical Personalities

1. Paul – "Paul the Apostle, commonly known as Saint Paul, was an eventual follower of Jesus (though not one of the Twelve Apostles) who professed the gospel of Christ to the first-century world. Paul is commonly regarded as one of the most influential figures of the Apostolic Age. He founded several churches in Asia Minor and Europe. He took advantage of his standing as both a Jew and a Roman citizen to counsel to both Jewish and Roman audiences. According to records in the New Testament and before his conversion, Paul was committed to persecuting the early followers of Jesus in the region of Jerusalem. In the account of the Acts of the Apostles (often indicated simply as Acts), Paul was traveling on the road from Jerusalem to Damascus with the purpose to "arrest them and bring them back to Jerusalem" when the resurrected Jesus appeared to him in a great light. He was struck blind, but after three days his sight was renewed by Ananias of Damascus and Paul began to preach that Jesus of Nazareth is the Jewish Messiah and the Son of God. Approximately half of the book of Acts deals with Paul's life and works."[6]

---

[6] "Paul in the Bible - His Life and Story," biblestudytools.com, accessed July 20, 2022, https://www.biblestudytools.com/topical-verses/paul-in-the-bible/.

2. "Silvanus is known in Acts by the shorter name Silas (Acts 15:22, 34, 40). A comparison of Acts 18:5 Corinthians 1:19 affirms the belief that Silvanus is another form of the name Silas.[7]

3. Timothy – "The mother of Timothy was a Jewess named Eunice. She later, however, became a Jewish Christian (Acts 16:1, 2Timothy 1:5). His father was a Greek (Gentile). The grandmother of Timothy, on his mother's side, was named Lois and she, too, became a Christian. Both women were likely converted during Paul's first evangelistic journey to the city in 46 A.D., when he healed a cripple man but soon after was stoned to death and resurrected (see Acts 14).

According to Paul, Timothy was taught about the Scriptures when he was a child (2Timothy 3:14 - 15). Note that the Old Testament, which many people disregard, was the foundation on which salvation could be achieved! The first time Paul meets an unmarried Timothy is in Lystra, around early 50 A.D., soon after he began his second missionary journey"[8]

Biblical Locations

1. Thessalonia

---

[7] 2 minute read, "Who Is Silvanus in the Bible? ," BibleAsk, June 3, 2022, https://bibleask.org/who-is-silvanus-in-the-bible/.

[8] "Home," Bible Study, accessed July 20, 2022, https://www.biblestudy.org/bible-study-by-topic/people-in-the-bible/timothy.html.

Thoughts

This chapter has a good explanation of what faith is all about. Paul defines faith as trusting that one will enter Heaven by living a life that emulates Yeshua. This is a very interesting and short way to explain faith. People who live following Yeshua's words and actions will enter Heaven at the end of their days. That is what faith in Yeshua is all about.

---

9 "Home," AwesomeStories, June 17, 2020, https://awesomestories.org/.

Chapter Two

Language

Peshitta in English	New American Standard 1995
1Th. 2:1 And ye yourselves, my brethren, know our entrance among you, that it was not in vain: [2] but we first suffered and were treated with indignity, as ye know, at Philippi; and then, in a great agony, with confidence in our God, we addressed to you the gospel of the Messiah. [3] For our exhortation proceeded not from deceit, nor from impurity, nor in guile: [4] but as we had been approved of God to be intrusted with the gospel, so we speak, not as pleasing men, but God who searcheth our hearts. [5] For at no time have we used flattering speech; as ye know; nor a cloak of cupidity, God is witness. [6] Neither have we sought glory from men, either from you or from others, when we might have been chargeable as legates of the Messiah. [7] But we were lowly among you; and like a nurse, who fondleth her children, [8] so we also fondled [you], and were desirous to impart to you, not the gospel of God merely, but also our own soul, because ye were dear to us. [9] For ye recollect, brethren, that we labored and toiled, working with our own hands, by night and by day, that we might not be chargeable to any one of you. [10] Ye are witnesses, and God [also], how we preached to you the gospel of God, purely, and uprightly, and were blameless towards all them that believe: [11] as yourselves know, we entreated each one	1Th. 2:1 For you yourselves know, brethren, that our [1a]coming to you [b]was not in vain, [2] but after we had already suffered and been [a]mistreated in [b]Philippi, as you know, we had the boldness in our God [c]to speak to you the [d]gospel of God amid much [1e]opposition. [3] For our [a]exhortation does not *come* from [b]error or [c]impurity or [1]by way of [d]deceit; [4] [a]but just as we have been approved by God to be [b]entrusted with the gospel, so we speak, [c]not as pleasing men, but God who [1d]examines our hearts. [5] For we never came [1]with flattering speech, as you know, nor with [a]a pretext for greed — [b]God is witness — [6] nor did we [a]seek glory from men, either from you or from others, even though as [b]apostles of Christ [1]we might have [2]asserted our authority. [7] But we [1]proved to be [2a]gentle [3]among you, [b]as a nursing *mother* [4]tenderly cares for her own children. [8] Having so fond an affection for you, we were well-pleased to [a]impart to you not only the [b]gospel of God but also our own [1]lives, because you had become [2]very dear to us. 1Th. 2:9 For you recall, brethren, our [a]labor and hardship, *how* [b]working night and day so as not to be a [c]burden to any of you, we proclaimed to you the [d]gospel of God. [10] You are witnesses, and *so is* [a]God, [b]how devoutly and uprightly and blamelessly we [1]behaved toward you

of you, as a father his children, and comforted your hearts: [12] and we charged you, to walk as it becometh God, who hath called you to his kingdom and his glory. [13] Therefore also we give thanks unceasingly to God, that the word of God which ye received from us, ye did not receive as the word of men, but as being truly the word of God, which worketh efficiently in you and in them that believe. [14] For ye, my brethren, became assimilated to the churches of God in Judaea, the persons who are in Jesus the Messiah; in that ye so suffered, even ye from your own countrymen, as also they from the Jews, [15] the persons who slew our Lord Jesus the Messiah, and persecuted their own prophets and us; and they please not God, and are made hostile to all men; [16] and they forbid us to speak to the Gentiles, that they may have life; to fill up their sins at all times. And wrath cometh on them to the uttermost. [17] But we, my brethren, have been bereaved of you for a short time, (in visible presence, not in our hearts,) and have the more exerted ourselves, to behold your faces, with great affection. [18] And we purposed to come to you, I Paul, once and again; but Satan hindered me. [19] For what is our hope, and our joy, and the crown of our glorying; unless it be ye, before our Lord Jesus at his coming? [20] For ye are our glory, and our joy.

[2]believers; [11] just as you know how we *were* [a]exhorting and encouraging and [1b]imploring each one of you as [c]a father *would* his own children, [12] so that you would [a]walk in a manner worthy of the God who [b]calls you into His own kingdom and [c]glory.

1Th. 2:13 For this reason we also constantly [a]thank God that when you received the [b]word of God which you heard from us, you accepted *it* [c]not *as* the word of men, but *for* what it really is, the word of God, [d]which also performs its work in you who believe. [14] For you, brethren, became [a]imitators of [b]the churches of God in Christ Jesus that are [c]in Judea, for [d]you also endured the same sufferings at the hands of your own countrymen, [e]even as they *did* from the Jews, [15] [a]who both killed the Lord Jesus and [b]the prophets, and [1]drove us out. [2]They are not pleasing to God, [2]but hostile to all men, [16] [a]hindering us from speaking to the Gentiles [b]so that they may be saved; with the result that they always [c]fill up the measure of their sins. But [d]wrath has come upon them [1]to the utmost.

1Th. 2:17 But we, brethren, having been taken away from you for a [1]short while — [a]in [2]person, not in [3]spirit — were all the more eager with great desire [b]to see your face. [18] [1]For [a]we wanted to come to you — I, Paul, [2b]more than once — and *yet* [c]Satan [d]hindered us. [19] For who is our hope or [a]joy or crown of exultation? Is it not even you, in the presence of our Lord Jesus at His [1b]coming? [20] For you are [a]our glory and joy.

References to the New American Standard 1995

1Thessalonians 2:1
[1]Lit *entrance*
[a]1 Thess 1:9
[b]2 Thess 1:10

1Thessalonians 2:2
[1]Or *struggle, conflict*
[a]Acts 14:5; 16:19-24; Phil 1:30
[b]Acts 16:22-24
[c]Acts 17:1-9
[d]Rom 1:1
[e]Phil 1:30

1Thessalonians 2:3
[1]Lit *in deceit*
[a]Acts 13:15
[b]2 Thess 2:11
[c]1 Thess 4:7
[d]2 Cor 4:2

1Thessalonians 2:4
[1]Or *approves*
[a]2 Cor 2:17
[b]Gal 2:7
[c]Gal 1:10
[d]Rom 8:27

1Thessalonians 2:5
[1]Lit *in a word of flattery*
[a]Acts 20:33; 2 Pet 2:3
[b]Rom 1:9; 1 Thess 2:10

1Thessalonians 2:6
[1]Lit *being able to*
[2]Or *be burdensome*
[a]John 5:41, 44; 2 Cor 4:5
[b]1 Cor 9:1f

1Thessalonians 2:7
[1]Or *became gentle*
[2]Three early mss read *babes*
[3]Lit *in the midst of you*
[4]Or *cherishes*
[a]2 Tim 2:24
[b]Gal 4:19; 1 Thess 2:11

1Thessalonians 2:8
[1]Or *souls*
[2]Lit *beloved*
[a]2 Cor 12:15; 1 John 3:16
[b]Rom 1:1

1Thessalonians 2:9
[a]Phil 4:16; 2 Thess 3:8
[b]Acts 18:3
[c]1 Cor 9:4f; 2 Cor 11:9
[d]Rom 1:1

1Thessalonians 2:10
[1]Lit *became*
[2]Or who *believe*
[a]1 Thess 2:5
[b]2 Cor 1:12; 1 Thess 1:5

1Thessalonians 2:11
[1]Or *testifying to*
[a]1 Thess 5:14
[b]Luke 16:28; 1 Thess 4:6
[c]1 Cor 4:14; 1 Thess 2:7

1Thessalonians 2:12
[a]Eph 4:1
[b]Rom 8:28; 1 Thess 5:24; 2 Thess 2:14
[c]2 Cor 4:6; 1 Pet 5:10

1Thessalonians 2:13
[a]Rom 1:8; 1 Thess 1:2
[b]Rom 10:17; Heb 4:2
[c]Matt 10:20; Gal 4:14
[d]Heb 4:12

1Thessalonians 2:14
[a]1 Thess 1:6
[b]1 Cor 7:17; 10:32
[c]Gal 1:22
[d]Acts 17:5; 1 Thess 3:4; 2 Thess 1:4f
[e]Heb 10:33f

1Thessalonians 2:15
[1]Or *persecuted us*
[2]Lit *and*
[a]Luke 24:20; Acts 2:23
[b]Matt 5:12; Acts 7:52

1Thessalonians 2:16
[1]Or *forever* or *altogether;* lit *to* the *end*
[a]Acts 9:23; 13:45, 50; 14:2, 5, 19; 17:5, 13; 18:12; 21:21f, 27; 25:2, 7
[b]1 Cor 10:33
[c]Gen 15:16; Dan 8:23; Matt 23:32
[d]1 Thess 1:10

1Thessalonians 2:17
[1]Lit *occasion of an hour*
[2]Lit *face*
[3]Lit *heart*
[a]1 Cor 5:3
[b]1 Thess 3:10

1Thessalonians 2:18
[1]Or *Because*
[2]Lit *both once and twice*
[a]Rom 15:22
[b]Phil 4:16
[c]Matt 4:10
[d]Rom 1:13; 15:22

1Thessalonians 2:19
[1]Or *presence*
[a]Phil 4:1
[b]Matt 16:27; Mark 8:38; John 21:22; 1 Thess 3:13; 4:15; 5:23

1Thessalonians 2:20
[a]2 Cor 1:14

Koine Greek

1Th. 2:1   Αυτοι γαρ οιδατε, αδελφοι, την εισοδον ημων την προς υμας, οτι ου κενη γεγονεν· ² αλλα προπαθοντες και υβρισθεντες, καθως οιδατε, εν Φιλιπποις, επαρρησιασαμεθα εν τω θεω ημων λαλησαι προς υμας το ευαγγελιον του θεου εν πολλω αγωνι. ³ Η γαρ παρακλησις ημων ουκ εκ πλανης, ουδε εξ ακαθαρσιας, ουτε εν δολω· ⁴ αλλα καθως δεδοκιμασμεθα υπο του θεου πιστευθηναι το ευαγγελιον, ουτως λαλουμεν, ουχ ως ανθρωποις αρεσκοντες, αλλα τω θεω τω δοκιμαζοντι τας καρδιας ημων. ⁵ Ουτε γαρ ποτε εν λογω κολακειας εγενηθημεν, καθως οιδατε, ουτε εν προφασει πλεονεξιας· θεος μαρτυς· ⁶ ουτε ζητουντες εξ ανθρωπων δοξαν, ουτε αφ' υμων ουτε απο αλλων, δυναμενοι εν βαρει ειναι, ως χριστου αποστολοι, ⁷ αλλ' εγενηθημεν ηπιοι εν μεσω υμων ως αν τροφος θαλπη τα εαυτης τεκνα· ⁸ ουτως, ομειρομενοι υμων, ευδοκουμεν μεταδουναι υμιν ου μονον το ευαγγελιον του θεου, αλλα και τας εαυτων ψυχας, διοτι αγαπητοι ημιν γεγενησθε. ⁹ Μνημονευετε γαρ, αδελφοι, τον κοπον ημων και τον μοχθον· νυκτος γαρ και ημερας εργαζομενοι, προς το μη επιβαρησαι τινα υμων, εκηρυξαμεν εις υμας το ευαγγελιον του θεου. ¹⁰ Υμεις μαρτυρες και ο θεος, ως οσιως και δικαιως και αμεμπτως υμιν τοις πιστευουσιν εγενηθημεν· ¹¹ καθαπερ οιδατε ως ενα εκαστον υμων, ως πατηρ τεκνα εαυτου, παρακαλουντες υμας και παραμυθουμενοι ¹² και μαρτυρομενοι, εις το περιπατησαι υμας αξιως του θεου του καλουντος υμας εις την εαυτου βασιλειαν και δοξαν.

1Th. 2:13   Δια τουτο και ημεις ευχαριστουμεν τω θεω αδιαλειπτως, οτι παραλαβοντες λογον ακοης παρ' ημων του θεου, εδεξασθε ου λογον ανθρωπων, αλλα καθως εστιν αληθως, λογον θεου, ος και ενεργειται εν υμιν τοις πιστευουσιν. ¹⁴ Υμεις γαρ μιμηται εγενηθητε, αδελφοι, των εκκλησιων του θεου των ουσων εν τη Ιουδαια εν χριστω Ιησου· οτι τα αυτα επαθετε και υμεις υπο των ιδιων συμφυλετων, καθως και αυτοι υπο των Ιουδαιων, ¹⁵ των και τον κυριον αποκτειναντων Ιησουν και τους ιδιους προφητας, και ημας εκδιωξαντων, και θεω μη αρεσκοντων, και πασιν ανθρωποις εναντιων, ¹⁶ κωλυοντων ημας τοις εθνεσιν λαλησαι ινα σωθωσιν, εις το αναπληρωσαι αυτων τας αμαρτιας παντοτε· εφθασεν δε επ' αυτους η οργη εις τελος.

1Th. 2:17   Ημεις δε, αδελφοι, απορφανισθεντες αφ' υμων προς καιρον ωρας, προσωπω ου καρδια, περισσοτερως εσπουδασαμεν το προσωπον υμων ιδειν εν πολλη επιθυμια· ¹⁸ διο ηθελησαμεν ελθειν προς υμας, εγω μεν Παυλος και απαξ και δις, και ενεκοψεν ημας ο Σατανας. ¹⁹ Τις γαρ ημων ελπις η χαρα η στεφανος καυχησεως; Η ουχι και υμεις, εμπροσθεν του κυριου ημων Ιησου εν τη αυτου παρουσια; ²⁰ Υμεις γαρ εστε η δοξα ημων και η χαρα.

Process of Discovery

Linguistics Section

Linguistic Structure

1. **²** but we first suffered and were treated with indignity, as ye know, at Philippi; and then, in a great agony, with confidence in our God, we addressed to you the gospel of the Messiah.

   Paul referred to Yeshua as the Messiah, indicating that this congregation was a group of Jews who believed that Yeshua was the Messiah.

2. **⁶** Neither have we sought glory from men, either from you or from others, when we might have been chargeable as legates of the Messiah.

   This verse shows that Paul refers to Yeshua as the Messiah, and not God. Therefore, this is additional proof that this congregation was a Jewish group who believed in Yeshua as the Messiah.

3. **¹⁴** For ye, my brethren, became assimilated to the churches of God in Judaea, the persons who are in Jesus the Messiah; in that ye so suffered, even ye from your own countrymen, as also they from the Jews,

   This verse supports the idea that the congregation was mostly comprised of Jewish worshipers.

The NASB 1995 was used for the chiastic structure.

A [1] For you yourselves know, brethren, that our [1a]coming to you [b]was not in vain, [2] but after we had already suffered and been [a]mistreated in [b]Philippi, as you know, we had the boldness in our God [c]to speak to you the [d]gospel of God amid much [1e]opposition. [3] For our [a]exhortation does not *come* from [b]error or [c]impurity or [1]by way of [d]deceit; [4] [a]but just as we have been approved by God to be [b]entrusted with the gospel, so we speak, [c]not as pleasing men, but God who [1d]examines our hearts. [5] For we never came [1]with flattering speech, as you know, nor with *a pretext for greed — *God is witness — **6** nor did we *seek glory from men, either from you or from others, even though as *apostles of Christ ¹we might have ²asserted our authority. **7** But we ¹proved to be ²*gentle ³among you, *as a nursing *mother* ⁴tenderly cares for her own children. **8** Having so fond an affection for you, we were well-pleased to *impart to you not only the *gospel of God but also our own ¹lives, because you had become ²very dear to us.

B⁹ For you recall, brethren, our *labor and hardship, *how* *working night and day so as not to be a *burden to any of you, we proclaimed to you the *gospel of God. **10** You are witnesses, and *so is* *God, *how devoutly and uprightly and blamelessly we ¹behaved toward you ²believers; **11** just as you know how we *were* *exhorting and encouraging and ¹*imploring each one of you as *a father *would* his own children, **12** so that you would *walk in a manner worthy of the God who *calls you into His own kingdom and *glory.

B' **13** For this reason we also constantly *thank God that when you received the *word of God which you heard from us, you accepted *it* *not *as* the word of men, but *for* what it really is, the word of God, *which also performs its work in you who believe. **14** For you, brethren, became *imitators of *the churches of God in Christ Jesus that are *in Judea, for *you also endured the same sufferings at the hands of your own countrymen, *even as they *did* from the Jews, **15** *who both killed the Lord Jesus and *the prophets, and ¹drove us out. ²They are not pleasing to God, ²but hostile to all men, **16** *hindering us from speaking to the Gentiles *so that they may be saved; with the result that they always *fill up the measure of their sins. But *wrath has come upon them ¹to the utmost.

A' **17** But we, brethren, having been taken away from you for a ¹short while — *in ²person, not in ³spirit — were all the more eager with great desire *to see your face. **18** ¹For *we wanted to come to you — I, Paul, ²*more than once — and *yet* *Satan *hindered us. **19** For who is our hope or *joy or crown of exultation? Is it not even you, in the presence of our Lord Jesus at His ¹*coming? **20** For you are *our glory and joy.

Discussion

Paul commends the congregation for their faith in Yeshua. Paul likes to remind the congregations he wrote to that he suffered to bring the Gospel message.

Questioning the narrative

1. What is the Gospel of God? (v. 10)

   Paul believed that Yeshua's Gospel, his message, was from the LORD.

2. Why was Paul bitter against Jews? (v. 14 & 15)

   Paul reminded the people in the congregation that they were linked to the churches in Judea. He told them that these Jewish believers in Yeshua suffered greatly. The center of Judaism was Jerusalem. From time to time, the High Priest would send letters or envoys to the synagogues to keep in touch with them and to remind them of his power. Paul had become bitter toward the Jewish High Priest and the Sanhedrin because of the way they treated him. He was concerned that the congregation could stop worshiping Yeshua because of pressure from Jerusalem.

Culture Section

Questioning the passage

1. What does it mean to have God as a witness? (v. 5)

   "God is a witness" is a Near Eastern expression that Semitic people used as a figure of speech. It was used when oral agreements were made. Very rarely were contracts written down. The Semitic people would say, "let God be a witness between us." When arguments occurred due to debts or deeds, Semites often said, "I have no witness but God," or "God is my witness."

   Two witnesses were required to be present when agreements and contracts were made. When no witnesses could be found, God was made a witness. "God as a witness" was equivalent to taking an oath in the name of the

LORD. In Semitic courts, when a case cannot be adjudicated, the party suspected of guilt was made to take an oath in the name of the LORD.

Paul told the congregation that God was a witness to his labors and trials to bring the Gospel message to them.[10]

2. What is a nursing mother? (v. 7)

A nursing mother is also referring to a foster mother. Foster parents were common in Paul's day. The practice originated because of polygamy. Rich men would have several wives and many children. It sometimes became impossible to raise so many children. Therefore, the children would be given to servants and trustworthy citizens who received remunerations for raising the children. The problem was that the children became attached to the foster parents and did not want to leave the foster parents' home. Paul said to the congregation that they must not get so attached to Paul that they forget that they belong to Yeshua.[11]

Thoughts

It was not easy to follow the ways of Yeshua in Paul's day. There was constant pressure from Jerusalem and from the Jews in the city who did not believe in Yeshua. The congregation was strong and kept Yeshua's ways during persecution. Paul tells them about his suffering and places the blame on Satan. Paul believed that Satan was trying to stop his efforts.

---

[10] Rocco A. Errico and George M. Lamsa, *Aramaic Light on Galatians through Hebrews: A Commentary Based on Aramaic, the Language of Jesus, and Ancient near Eastern Customs* (Smyma, GA: Noohra Foundation, 2005).
[11] IBID.

Chapter Three

Language

Peshitta in English	New American Standard 1995
1Th. 3:1 And, because we could no longer endure it, we were willing to be left alone at Athens, ² and to send to you Timothy our brother, a servant of God, and our assistant in the announcement of the Messiah; that he might strengthen you, and inquire of you respecting your faith: ³ lest any of you should be disheartened by these afflictions; for ye know, that we are appointed thereto. ⁴ For also when we were with you, we forewarned you, that we were to be afflicted; as ye know did occur. ⁵ Therefore also I could not be quiet, until I sent to learn your faith; lest the Tempter should have tempted you, and our labor have been in vain. ⁶ But now, since Timothy hath come to us from among you, and hath informed us respecting your faith and your love, and that ye have a good remembrance of us at all times, and that ye desire to see us, even as we [to see] you; ⁷ therefore we are comforted in you, my brethren, amid all our straits and afflictions, on account of your faith. ⁸ And now, we live, if ye stand fast in our Lord. ⁹ For what thanks can we render to God in your behalf, for all the joy with which we are joyful on your account; ¹⁰ unless it be, that we the more supplicate before God, by night and by day, that we may see your faces, and may perfect what is lacking in your faith? ¹¹ And may God our Father, and our Lord Jesus the Messiah, direct our way unto	1Th. 3:1 Therefore ^awhen we could endure *it* no longer, we thought it best to be left behind at ^bAthens alone, ² and we sent ^aTimothy, our brother and God's fellow worker in the gospel of Christ, to strengthen and encourage you as to your faith, ³ so that no one would be ¹disturbed by these afflictions; for you yourselves know that ^awe have been destined for this. ⁴ For indeed when we were with you, we *kept* telling you in advance that we were going to suffer affliction; ^{1a}and so it came to pass, ²as you know. ⁵ For this reason, ^awhen I could endure *it* no longer, I also ^bsent to ¹find out about your faith, for fear that ^cthe tempter might have tempted you, and ^dour labor would be in vain. 1Th. 3:6 But now that ^aTimothy has come to us from you, and has brought us good news of ^byour faith and love, and that you always ^cthink kindly of us, longing to see us just as we also long to see you, ⁷ for this reason, brethren, in all our distress and affliction we were comforted about you through your faith; ⁸ for now we *really* live, if you ^astand firm in the Lord. ⁹ For ^awhat thanks can we render to God for you in return for all the joy with which we rejoice before our God on your account, ¹⁰ as we ^anight and day keep praying most earnestly that we may

you; [12] and increase and enlarge your love towards one another, and towards all men, even as we love you; [13] and establish your hearts unblamable in holiness, before God our Father; at the advent of our Lord Jesus the Messiah, with all his saints.	[b]see your face, and may [c]complete what is lacking in your faith? 1Th. 3:11 [a]Now may [b]our God and Father [c]Himself and Jesus our Lord [d]direct our way to you; [12] and may the Lord cause you to increase and [a]abound in love for one another, and for all people, just as we also *do* for you; [13] so that He may [a]establish your hearts [b]without blame in holiness before [c]our God and Father at the [1d]coming of our Lord Jesus [e]with all His [2]saints.

References to the New American Standard 1995

1 Thessalonians 3:1
[a]1 Thess 3:5
[b]Acts 17:15f

1 Thessalonians 3:2
[a]2 Cor 1:1; Col 1:1

1 Thessalonians 3:3
[1]Or *deceived*
[a]Acts 9:16; 14:22

1 Thessalonians 3:4
[1]Lit *just as*
[2]Lit *and*
[a]1 Thess 2:14

1 Thessalonians 3:5
[1]Or *to know, to ascertain*
[a]Phil 2:19; 1 Thess 3:1
[b]1 Thess 3:2
[c]Matt 4:3
[d]2 Cor 6:1; Phil 2:16

1 Thessalonians 3:6
[a]Acts 18:5
[b]1 Thess 1:3
[c]1 Cor 11:2

1 Thessalonians 3:8
[a]1 Cor 16:13

1 Thessalonians 3:9
[a]1 Thess 1:2

1 Thessalonians 3:10
[a]2 Tim 1:3
[b]1 Thess 2:17
[c]2 Cor 13:9

1Thessalonians 3:11

[a]2 Thess 2:16
[b]Gal 1:4; 1 Thess 3:13
[c]1 Thess 4:16; 5:23; 2 Thess 2:16; 3:16; Rev 21:3
[d]2 Thess 3:5

1Thessalonians 3:12

[a]Phil 1:9; 1 Thess 4:1, 10; 2 Thess 1:3

1Thessalonians 3:13

[1]Or *presence*
[2]Or *holy ones*
[a]1 Cor 1:8; 1 Thess 3:2
[b]Luke 1:6
[c]Gal 1:4; 1 Thess 3:11
[d]1 Thess 2:19
[e]Matt 25:31; Mark 8:38; 1 Thess 4:17; 2 Thess 1:7

Koine Greek

1Th. 3:1   Διο μηκετι στεγοντες, ευδοκησαμεν καταλειφθηναι εν Αθηναις μονοι, ² και επεμψαμεν Τιμοθεον τον αδελφον ημων και διακονον του θεου και συνεργον ημων εν τω ευαγγελιω του χριστου, εις το στηριξαι υμας και παρακαλεσαι υμας περι της πιστεως υμων, ³ το μηδενα σαινεσθαι εν ταις θλιψεσιν ταυταις· αυτοι γαρ οιδατε οτι εις τουτο κειμεθα. ⁴ Και γαρ οτε προς υμας ημεν, προελεγομεν υμιν οτι μελλομεν θλιβεσθαι, καθως και εγενετο και οιδατε. ⁵ Δια τουτο καγω, μηκετι στεγων, επεμψα εις το γνωναι την πιστιν υμων, μηπως επειρασεν υμας ο πειραζων, και εις κενον γενηται ο κοπος ημων. ⁶ Αρτι δε ελθοντος Τιμοθεου προς ημας αφ᾽ υμων, και ευαγγελισαμενου ημιν την πιστιν και την αγαπην υμων, και οτι εχετε μνειαν ημων αγαθην παντοτε, επιποθουντες ημας ιδειν, καθαπερ και ημεις υμας· ⁷ δια τουτο παρεκληθημεν, αδελφοι, εφ᾽ υμιν επι παση τη θλιψει και αναγκη ημων δια της υμων πιστεως· ⁸ οτι νυν ζωμεν, εαν υμεις στηκετε εν κυριω. ⁹ Τινα γαρ ευχαριστιαν δυναμεθα τω θεω ανταποδουναι περι υμων, επι παση τη χαρα η χαιρομεν δι᾽ υμας εμπροσθεν του θεου ημων, ¹⁰ νυκτος και ημερας υπερ εκπερισσου δεομενοι εις το ιδειν υμων το προσωπον, και καταρτισαι τα υστερηματα της πιστεως υμων;

1Th. 3:11   Αυτος δε ο θεος και πατηρ ημων, και ο κυριος ημων Ιησους χριστος, κατευθυναι την οδον ημων προς υμας· ¹² υμας δε ο κυριος πλεονασαι και περισσευσαι τη αγαπη εις αλληλους και εις παντας, καθαπερ και ημεις εις υμας, ¹³ εις το στηριξαι υμων τας καρδιας αμεμπτους εν αγιωσυνη, εμπροσθεν του θεου και πατρος ημων, εν τη παρουσια του κυριου ημων Ιησου χριστου μετα παντων των αγιων αυτου.

Process of Discovery

Linguistics Section

Linguistic Structure

1. [11] And may God our Father, and our Lord Jesus the Messiah, direct our way unto you

   Paul demonstrated this is a Jewish congregation by giving Yeshua the title of Messiah, not God.

2. [13] and establish your hearts unblamable in holiness, before God our Father; at the advent of our Lord Jesus the Messiah, with all his saints.

   Again Paul shows his belief in Yeshua as the Messiah and not divine.

The NASB 1995 was used for the chiastic structure.

[Paul in Athens] 1Th. 3:1   Therefore [a]when we could endure *it* no longer, we thought it best to be left behind at [b]Athens alone, [2] and we sent [a]Timothy, our brother and God's fellow worker in the gospel of Christ, to strengthen and encourage you as to your faith, [3] so that no one would be [1]disturbed by these afflictions; for you yourselves know that [a]we have been destined for this. [4] For indeed when we were with you, we *kept* telling you in advance that we were going to suffer affliction; [1a]and so it came to pass, [2]as you know. [5] For this reason, [a]when I could endure *it* no longer, I also [b]sent to [1]find out about your faith, for fear that [c]the tempter might have tempted you, and [d]our labor would be in vain.

[A message to the congregation] 1Th. 3:6   But now that [a]Timothy has come to us from you, and has brought us good news of [b]your faith and love, and that you always [c]think kindly of us, longing to see us just as we also long to see you, [7] for this reason, brethren, in all our distress and affliction we were comforted about you through your faith; [8] for now we *really* live, if you [a]stand firm in the Lord. [9] For [a]what thanks can we render to God for you in return for all the joy with which we rejoice before our God on your account, [10] as we [a]night and day keep praying most earnestly that we may [b]see your face, and may [c]complete what is lacking in your faith?

[A blessing] 1Th. 3:11   *a*Now may *b*our God and Father *c*Himself and Jesus our Lord *d*direct our way to you; *12* and may the Lord cause you to increase and *a*abound in love for one another, and for all people, just as we also *do* for you; *13* so that He may *a*establish your hearts *b*without blame in holiness before *c*our God and Father at the *1d*coming of our Lord Jesus *c*with all His *2*saints.

Discussion

In this chapter, Paul warns the congregation that they should not listen to anyone who preaches a different view of Yeshua than his.

Culture Section

Discussion

Paul was concerned that other missionaries for Yeshua would arrive at the congregations that he established. Paul believed he had the only message and methodology about having faith in Yeshua the Messiah. His biggest opponent was the Gnostic Christians from north Egypt. Other Christian expressions were formed during Paul's lifetime. So, Paul constantly warned the congregations to look for the "false teachers." The world would be completely different today if the Gnostic Christians survived instead of the proto-orthodox Christians.

Questioning the passage

1. What does "now, we life?" (v. 8)

   This phrase is a Near Eastern expression meaning, "now we rejoice."[12]

---

[12] Rocco A. Errico and George M. Lamsa, *Aramaic Light on Galatians through Hebrews: A Commentary Based on Aramaic, the Language of Jesus, and Ancient near Eastern Customs* (Smyma, GA: Noohra Foundation, 2005).

Thoughts

It is essential when deciding on a community of Christians to join to determine what they believe. In Christianity, there are over 1000 denominations. The best thing to do is ask the church for their faith statement and doctrinal statement. What does the church believe, and what traditions do they follow. One thing that occurred from the beginning of the Yeshua movement was the church's difference of opinion and splintering. Paul and Peter saw things differently. In 48 C.E., they agreed on what a Yeshua follower had to do. Paul left that meeting with an agreement, tossed it in the trash heap, and did his own thing. Mainline and independent churches are doing that today. So, what is the expression of faith in Yeshua? Religion is supposed to define that for us. However, it does not. Most churches are interested in their power over your life and wealth. The recommendation is to have the church officers show where in the Bible their actions are defined. Then use your knowledge of the Bible to determine if their explanations are correct.

Chapter Four

Language

Peshitta in English	New American Standard 1995
1Th. 4:1 Wherefore, my brethren, I entreat you, and beseech you by our Lord Jesus, that, as ye have received from us how ye ought to walk, and to please God, so ye would make progress more and more. [2] For ye know what command we gave you in our Lord Jesus the Messiah. [3] For this is the pleasure of God, your sanctification; and that ye be separated from all whoredom; [4] and that each one of you might know how to possess his vessel, in sanctity and in honor; [5] and not in the concupiscence of lust, like the rest of the Gentiles who know not God: [6] and that ye dare not to transgress and to overreach any one his brother, in this matter; because our Lord is the avenger of all these, as also we have said and testified to you in time past. [7] For God did not call you unto impurity, but to sanctification. [8] He therefore who spurneth, spurneth not man but God, who hath given his Holy Spirit in you. [9] Now concerning love to the brethren, ye need not that I should write to you; for ye yourselves are taught of God to love one another. [10] Ye likewise do so, to all the brethren who are in all Macedonia: but I entreat you, my brethren, to be exuberant: [11] and that ye strive to be quiet, and to attend to your own affairs; and that ye labor with your own hands; as we directed you; [12] and that ye walk	1Th. 4:1 *a*Finally then, *b*brethren, we request and exhort you in the Lord Jesus, that as you received from us *instruction* as to how you ought to [1c]walk and *d*please God (just as you actually do [1]walk), that you *e*excel still more. [2] For you know what commandments we gave you [1]by *the authority of* the Lord Jesus. [3] For this is the will of God, your sanctification; *that is,* that you *a*abstain from [1]sexual immorality; [4] that *a*each of you know how to [1]possess his own [2b]vessel in sanctification and *c*honor, [5] not in [1a]lustful passion, like the Gentiles who *b*do not know God; [6] *and* that no man transgress and *a*defraud his brother *b*in the matter because *c*the Lord is *the* avenger in all these things, just as we also *d*told you before and solemnly warned *you*. [7] For *a*God has not called us for *b*the purpose of impurity, but [1]in sanctification. [8] So, he who rejects *this* is not rejecting man but the God who *a*gives His Holy Spirit to you. 1Th. 4:9 Now as to the *a*love of the brethren, you *b*have no need for *anyone* to write to you, for you yourselves are *c*taught by God to love one another; [10] for indeed *a*you do practice it toward all the brethren who are in all Macedonia. But we urge you, brethren, to *b*excel still more, [11] and to make it your ambition *a*to lead a quiet life and *b*attend to your own

becomingly towards those without; and that ye be dependent on no man. **13** And, I wish you to know, my brethren, that ye should not mourn over them who have fallen asleep, like other people who have no hope. **14** For if we believe that Jesus died and rose again, even so them who sleep, will God, by Jesus, bring with him. **15** And this we say to you, by the word of our Lord, that we who may survive and be alive, at the coming of our Lord, shall not precede them who have slept. **16** Because our Lord will himself descend from heaven, with the mandate, and with the voice of the chief angel, and with the trump of God; and the dead who are in the Messiah, will first arise; **17** and then, we who survive and are alive shall be caught up together with them to the clouds, to meet our Lord in the air; and so shall we be ever with our Lord. **18** Wherefore, comfort ye one another with these words.

business and [c]work with your hands, just as we commanded you, **12** so that you will [1a]behave properly toward [b]outsiders and [2c]not be in any need.

1Th. 4:13 But [a]we do not want you to be uninformed, brethren, about those who [b]are asleep, so that you will not grieve as do [c]the rest who have [d]no hope. **14** For if we believe that Jesus died and rose again, [a]even so God will bring with Him [b]those who have fallen asleep [1]in Jesus. **15** For this we say to you [a]by the word of the Lord, that [b]we who are alive [1]and remain until [c]the coming of the Lord, will not precede [d]those who have fallen asleep. **16** For the Lord [a]Himself [b]will descend from heaven with a [1c]shout, with the voice of [d]*the* archangel and with the [e]trumpet of God, and [f]the dead in Christ will rise first. **17** Then [a]we who are alive [1]and remain will be [b]caught up together with them [c]in the clouds to meet the Lord in the air, and so we shall always [d]be with the Lord. **18** Therefore comfort one another with these words.

References to the New American Standard 1995

1Thessalonians 4:1
[1]Or *conduct yourselves*
[a]2 Cor 13:11; 2 Thess 3:1
[b]Gal 6:1; 1 Thess 5:12; 2 Thess 1:3; 2:1; 3:1, 13
[c]Eph 4:1
[d]2 Cor 5:9
[e]Phil 1:9; 1 Thess 3:12; 4:10; 2 Thess 1:3

1Thessalonians 4:2
[1]Lit *through the Lord*

1Thessalonians 4:3
[1]Or *fornication*
[a]1 Cor 6:18

1Thessalonians 4:4
[1]Or *acquire*
[2]I.e. body; or wife
[a]1 Cor 7:2, 9
[b]2 Cor 4:7; 1 Pet 3:7
[c]Rom 1:24

1Thessalonians 4:5
[1]Lit *passion of lust*
[a]Rom 1:26
[b]Gal 4:8

1Thessalonians 4:6
[a]1 Cor 6:8
[b]2 Cor 7:11
[c]Rom 12:19; 13:4; Heb 13:4
[d]Luke 16:28; 1 Thess 2:11; Heb 2:6

1Thessalonians 4:7
[1]I.e. in the state or sphere of
[a]1 Pet 1:15
[b]1 Thess 2:3

1Thessalonians 4:8
[a]Rom 5:5; 2 Cor 1:22; Gal 4:6; 1 John 3:24

1Thessalonians 4:9
[a]John 13:34; Rom 12:10
[b]2 Cor 9:1; 1 Thess 5:1
[c]Jer 31:33f; John 6:45; 1 John 2:27

1Thessalonians 4:10
[a]1 Thess 1:7
[b]1 Thess 3:12

1Thessalonians 4:11
[a]2 Thess 3:12
[b]1 Pet 4:15
[c]Acts 18:3; Eph 4:28; 2 Thess 3:10-12

1Thessalonians 4:12
[1]Lit *walk*
[2]Lit *have need of nothing*
[a]Rom 13:13; Col 4:5
[b]Mark 4:11
[c]Eph 4:28

1Thessalonians 4:13
[a]Rom 1:13
[b]Acts 7:60
[c]Eph 2:3; 1 Thess 5:6
[d]Eph 2:12

1Thessalonians 4:14
[1]Lit *through*
[a]Rom 14:9; 2 Cor 4:14
[b]1 Cor 15:18; 1 Thess 4:13

1Thessalonians 4:15
[1]Lit *who*
[a]1 Kin 13:17f; 20:35; 2 Cor 12:1; Gal 1:12
[b]1 Cor 15:52; 1 Thess 5:10
[c]1 Thess 2:19
[d]1 Cor 15:18; 1 Thess 4:13

1Thessalonians 4:16

[1]Or *cry of command*
[a]1 Thess 3:11
[b]1 Thess 1:10; 2 Thess 1:7
[c]Joel 2:11
[d]Jude 9
[e]Matt 24:31
[f]1 Cor 15:23; 2 Thess 2:1; Rev 14:13

1Thessalonians 4:17

[1]Lit *who*
[a]1 Cor 15:52; 1 Thess 5:10
[b]2 Cor 12:2
[c]Dan 7:13; Acts 1:9; Rev 11:12
[d]John 12:26

Koine Greek

1Th. 4:1   ⌐ Λοιπον ¬ ουν, αδελφοι, ερωτωμεν υμας και παρακαλουμεν εν κυριω Ιησου καθως παρελαβετε παρ' ημων το πως δει υμας περιπατειν και αρεσκειν θεω, ινα περισσευητε μαλλον. ² Οιδατε γαρ τινας παραγγελιας εδωκαμεν υμιν δια του κυριου Ιησου. ³ Τουτο γαρ εστιν θελημα του θεου, ο αγιασμος υμων, απεχεσθαι υμας απο της πορνειας· ⁴ ειδεναι εκαστον υμων το εαυτου σκευος κτασθαι εν αγιασμω και τιμη, ⁵ μη εν παθει επιθυμιας, καθαπερ και τα εθνη τα μη ειδοτα τον θεον· ⁶ το μη υπερβαινειν και πλεονεκτειν εν τω πραγματι τον αδελφον αυτου· διοτι εκδικος ο κυριος περι παντων τουτων, καθως και ⌐ προειπομεν ¬ υμιν και διεμαρτυραμεθα. ⁷ Ου γαρ εκαλεσεν ημας ο θεος επι ακαθαρσια, αλλ' εν αγιασμω. ⁸ Τοιγαρουν ο αθετων ουκ ανθρωπον αθετει, αλλα τον θεον τον και δοντα το πνευμα αυτου το αγιον εις υμας.

1Th. 4:9   Περι δε της φιλαδελφιας ου χρειαν εχετε γραφειν υμιν· αυτοι γαρ υμεις θεοδιδακτοι εστε εις το αγαπαν αλληλους· ¹⁰ και γαρ ποιειτε αυτο εις παντας τους αδελφους τους εν ολη τη Μακεδονια. Παρακαλουμεν δε υμας, αδελφοι, περισσευειν μαλλον, ¹¹ και φιλοτιμεισθαι ησυχαζειν, και πρασσειν τα ιδια, και εργαζεσθαι ταις ιδιαις χερσιν υμων, καθως υμιν παρηγγειλαμεν· ¹² ινα περιπατητε ευσχημονως προς τους εξω, και μηδενος χρειαν εχητε.

1Th. 4:13   Ου θελομεν δε υμας αγνοειν, αδελφοι, περι των κεκοιμημενων, ινα μη λυπησθε, καθως και οι λοιποι οι μη εχοντες ελπιδα. ¹⁴ Ει γαρ πιστευομεν οτι Ιησους απεθανεν και ανεστη, ουτως και ο θεος τους κοιμηθεντας δια του Ιησου αξει συν αυτω. ¹⁵ Τουτο γαρ υμιν λεγομεν εν λογω κυριου, οτι ημεις οι ζωντες οι περιλειπομενοι εις την παρουσιαν του κυριου, ου μη φθασωμεν τους κοιμηθεντας. ¹⁶ Οτι αυτος ο κυριος εν κελευσματι, εν φωνη αρχαγγελου, και εν σαλπιγγι θεου, καταβησεται απ' ουρανου, και οι νεκροι εν χριστω αναστησονται πρωτον· ¹⁷ επειτα ημεις οι ζωντες, οι περιλειπομενοι, αμα συν αυτοις αρπαγησομεθα εν νεφελαις εις απαντησιν του κυριου εις αερα· και ουτω παντοτε συν κυριω εσομεθα. ¹⁸ Ωστε παρακαλειτε αλληλους εν τοις λογοις τουτοις.

Process of Discovery

Linguistics Section

Linguistic Structure

1. [2] For ye know what command we gave you in our Lord Jesus the Messiah.

Paul continues to say that Yeshua was the Messiah and not divine.

The NASB 1995 was used for the chiastic structure.

[A life pleasing to the LORD] 1Th. 4:1 [a]Finally then, [b]brethren, we request and exhort you in the Lord Jesus, that as you received from us *instruction* as to how you ought to [1c]walk and [d]please God (just as you actually do [1]walk), that you [e]excel still more. [2] For you know what commandments we gave you [1]by *the authority of* the Lord Jesus. [3] For this is the will of God, your sanctification; *that is,* that you [a]abstain from [1]sexual immorality; [4] that [a]each of you know how to [1]possess his own [2b]vessel in sanctification and [c]honor, [5] not in [1d]lustful passion, like the Gentiles who [b]do not know God; [6] *and* that no man transgress and [a]defraud his brother [b]in the matter because [c]the Lord is *the* avenger in all these things, just as we also [d]told you before and solemnly warned *you.* [7] For [a]God has not called us for [b]the purpose of impurity, but [1]in sanctification. [8] So, he who rejects *this* is not rejecting man but the God who [a]gives His Holy Spirit to you. [9] Now as to the [a]love of the brethren, you [b]have no need for *anyone* to write to you, for you yourselves are [c]taught by God to love one another; [10] for indeed [a]you do practice it toward all the brethren who are in all Macedonia. But we urge you, brethren, to [b]excel still more, [11] and to make it your ambition [a]to lead a quiet life and [b]attend to your own business and [c]work with your hands, just as we commanded you, [12] so that you will [1a]behave properly toward [b]outsiders and [2c]not be in any need.

[Resurrection of the dead] 1Th. 4:13 But [a]we do not want you to be uninformed, brethren, about those who [b]are asleep, so that you will not grieve as do [c]the rest who have [d]no hope. [14] For if we believe that Jesus died and rose again, [a]even so God will bring with Him [b]those who have fallen asleep [1]in Jesus. [15] For this we say to you [a]by the word of the Lord, that [b]we who are alive [1]and remain until [c]the coming of the Lord, will not precede [d]those who have fallen asleep. [16] For the Lord [a]Himself [b]will descend from heaven with a [1c]shout, with the voice of [d]*the* archangel and with the [e]trumpet of God, and [f]the dead in Christ will rise first. [17] Then [a]we who are alive [1]and remain will be

^bcaught up together with them ^cin the clouds to meet the Lord in the air, and so we shall always ^dbe with the Lord. ¹⁸ Therefore comfort one another with these words.

Discussion

This chapter covers two topics. The first is a life pleasing to the LORD. The second has to do with the resurrection of people who died before the first coming of Yeshua.

Questioning the narrative

1. What does it mean to possess one's vessel in sanctification? (v. 4)

   This verse gave the church the idea that one's body is a vessel for God. The term "vessel" refers to the human body. Paul tells the congregation to follow and observe the commandments of Yeshua. They were to consider their bodies as sacred vessels. Sacred vessels were in the Temple in Jerusalem. Those vessels were sanctified for the LORD's use, and the people should consider themselves as sanctified vessels.[13]

Culture Section

Questioning the passage

1. What does it mean that the people "asleep" would meet Yeshua? (v. 15)

   The term "asleep" means dead. Paul believed that Yeshua was to return before he died. When that happened, the people who died before Yeshua lived would be resurrected from the dead.

2. What does it mean to "meet in the air/clouds?" (v. 16 & 17)

---

[13] Rocco A. Errico and George M. Lamsa, *Aramaic Light on Galatians through Hebrews: A Commentary Based on Aramaic, the Language of Jesus, and Ancient near Eastern Customs* (Smyma, GA: Noohra Foundation, 2005).

"Meet in the air" is an Aramaic idiom that means people will hasten to meet him before he sets his foot on the ground. This is a metaphoric description of how Yeshua was to return. Paul believed that Yeshua would return in a spiritual body so that all the world would be able to perceive him as the Messiah.[14]

Thoughts

Paul believed that Yeshua would return in his lifetime. Therefore, Paul saw it as imperative that he spread the Gospel as quickly as possible. Perhaps in his haste he got a few things incorrect. After trying to convert Jews he moved to the Gentiles. He converted Mithras House churches into Yeshua House churches. He did this with much haste. He believed that every person who he turned to Yeshua was another person saved from Satan. As it turns out Yeshua did not return and many of the pagan ways of Mithras are a cornerstone of today's Christian theology and doctrine (refer to my book "Christianity's Need for Mithras).

---

[14] IBID.

Chapter Five

Language

Peshitta in English	New American Standard 1995
1Th. 5:1 But concerning the times and seasons, my brethren, ye need not that I write to you: [2] for ye know assuredly, that the day of our Lord so cometh, as a thief by night. [3] While they will be saying, Peace and quietness, then suddenly destruction will burst upon them, as distress upon a child-bearer, and they will not escape. [4] But ye, my brethren, are not in darkness, that that day should overtake you as a thief. [5] For ye are all children of the light, and children of the day; and are not children of the night, and children of darkness. [6] Let us not therefore sleep, like others; but let us be vigilant and considerate. [7] For they who sleep, sleep in the night; and they who are drunken, are drunken in the night. [8] But let us who are children of the day, be wakeful in mind, and put on the breastplate of faith and love, and take the helmet of the hope of life. [9] For God hath not appointed us to wrath, but to the acquisition of life, by our Lord Jesus the Messiah: [10] who died for us, that whether we wake or sleep, we might live together with him. [11] Therefore comfort one another, and edify one another, as also ye have done. [12] And we entreat you, my brethren, that ye recognize them who labor among you, and who stand before your faces in our Lord, and instruct you: [13] that they may be esteemed by you with abundant love; and, on account of their work, live ye in	1Th. 5:1 Now as to the [a]times and the epochs, brethren, you [b]have no need of anything to be written to you. [2] For you yourselves know full well that [a]the day of the Lord [1]will come [b]just like a thief in the night. [3] While they are saying, "[a]Peace and safety!" then [1b]destruction [2]will come upon them suddenly like [c]labor pains upon a woman with child, and they will not escape. [4] But you, brethren, are not in [a]darkness, that the day would overtake you [1b]like a thief; [5] for you are all [a]sons of light and sons of day. We are not of night nor of [b]darkness; [6] so then let us not [a]sleep as [1b]others do, but let us be alert and [2c]sober. [7] For those who sleep do their sleeping at night, and those who get drunk get [a]drunk at night. [8] But since [a]we are of *the* day, let us [b]be [1]sober, having put on the [c]breastplate of [d]faith and love, and as a [e]helmet, the [f]hope of salvation. [9] For God has not destined us for [a]wrath, but for [b]obtaining salvation through our Lord Jesus Christ, [10] [a]who died for us, so that whether we are awake or asleep, we will live together with Him. [11] Therefore [1]encourage one another and [a]build up one another, just as you also are doing. 1Th. 5:12 But we request of you, brethren, that you [1a]appreciate those [b]who diligently labor among you, and [c]have charge over you in the Lord and

harmony with them. **14** And we entreat you, my brethren, that ye admonish the faulty, and encourage the faint-hearted, and bear the burdens of the weak, and be long suffering towards all men. **15** And beware, lest any of you return evil for evil, but always follow good deeds, towards one another, and towards all men. **16** And be joyful always. **17** And pray without ceasing. **18** And in every thing be thankful: For this is the pleasure of God in Jesus the Messiah, concerning you. **19** Quench not the Spirit. **20** Despise not prophesying. **21** Explore every thing, and hold fast the good: **22** and fly from every thing evil. **23** And may the God of peace sanctify you all, perfectly, and keep blameless your whole spirit, and your soul, and your body, till the coming of our Lord Jesus the Messiah. **24** Faithful is he that hath called you, who will do it. **25** My brethren, pray for us. **26** Salute all our brethren with a holy kiss. **27** I conjure you by our Lord, that this epistle be read to all the holy brethren. **28** The grace of our Lord Jesus the Messiah be with you. Amen.

give you [2]instruction, **13** and that you esteem them very highly in love because of their work. [a]Live in peace with one another. **14** We urge you, brethren, admonish [a]the [1]unruly, encourage [b]the fainthearted, help [c]the weak, be [d]patient with everyone. **15** See that [a]no one repays another with evil for evil, but always [b]seek after that which is good for one another and for all people. **16** [a]Rejoice always; **17** [a]pray without ceasing; **18** in everything [a]give thanks; for this is God's will for you in Christ Jesus. **19** [a]Do not quench the Spirit; **20** do not despise [a]prophetic [1]utterances. **21** But [a]examine everything *carefully;* [b]hold fast to that which is good; **22** abstain from every [1]form of evil.

1Th. 5:23   Now [a]may the God of peace [b]Himself sanctify you entirely; and may your [c]spirit and soul and body be preserved complete, [d]without blame at [e]the coming of our Lord Jesus Christ. **24** [a]Faithful is He who [b]calls you, and He also will bring it to pass.

1Th. 5:25   Brethren, [a]pray for us[1].

1Th. 5:26   [a]Greet all the brethren with a holy kiss. **27** I adjure you by the Lord to [a]have this letter read to all the [b]brethren.

1Th. 5:28   [a]The grace of our Lord Jesus Christ be with you.

References to the New American Standard 1995

1Thessalonians 5:1
*a*Acts 1:7
*b*1 Thess 4:9

1Thessalonians 5:2
¹Lit *is coming*
*a*1 Cor 1:8
*b*Luke 21:34; 1 Thess 5:4; 2 Pet 3:10; Rev 3:3; 16:15

1Thessalonians 5:3
¹Or *sudden destruction*
²Lit *comes upon*
*a*Jer 6:14; 8:11; Ezek 13:10
*b*2 Thess 1:9
*c*John 16:21

1Thessalonians 5:4
¹One early ms reads *like thieves*
*a*Acts 26:18; 1 John 2:8
*b*Luke 21:34; 1 Thess 5:2; 2 Pet 3:10; Rev 3:3; 16:15

1Thessalonians 5:5
*a*Luke 16:8
*b*Acts 26:18; 1 John 2:8

1Thessalonians 5:6
¹Lit *the remaining ones*
²Or *self-controlled*
*a*Rom 13:11; 1 Thess 5:10
*b*Eph 2:3; 1 Thess 4:13
*c*1 Pet 1:13

1Thessalonians 5:6
¹Lit *the remaining ones*
²Or *self-controlled*
*a*Rom 13:11; 1 Thess 5:10
*b*Eph 2:3; 1 Thess 4:13
*c*1 Pet 1:13

1Thessalonians 5:7
[a]Acts 2:15; 2 Pet 2:13

1Thessalonians 5:8
[1]Or *self-controlled*
[a]1 Thess 5:5
[b]1 Pet 1:13
[c]Is 59:17; Eph 6:14
[d]Eph 6:23
[e]Eph 6:17
[f]Rom 8:24

1Thessalonians 5:9
[a]1 Thess 1:10
[b]2 Thess 2:13f

1Thessalonians 5:10
[a]Rom 14:9

1Thessalonians 5:11
[1]Or *comfort*
[a]Eph 4:29

1Thessalonians 5:12
[1]Lit *know*
[2]Or *admonition*
[a]1 Cor 16:18; 1 Tim 5:17
[b]Rom 16:6, 12; 1 Cor 15:10; 16:16
[c]Heb 13:17

1Thessalonians 5:13
[a]Mark 9:50

1Thessalonians 5:14
[1]Or *undisciplined*
[a]2 Thess 3:6, 7, 11
[b]Is 35:4
[c]Rom 14:1f; 1 Cor 8:7ff; Rom 15:1
[d]1 Cor 13:4

1Thessalonians 5:15
[a]Matt 5:44; Rom 12:17; 1 Pet 3:9
[b]Rom 12:9; Gal 6:10; 1 Thess 5:21

1Thessalonians 5:16
[a]Phil 4:4

1Thessalonians 5:17
[a]Eph 6:18

1Thessalonians 5:18
[a]Eph 5:20

1Thessalonians 5:19
[a]Eph 4:30

1Thessalonians 5:20
[1]Or *gifts*
[a]Acts 13:1; 1 Cor 14:31

1Thessalonians 5:21
[a]1 Cor 14:29; 1 John 4:1
[b]Rom 12:9; Gal 6:10; 1 Thess 5:15

1Thessalonians 5:22
[1]Or *appearance*

1Thessalonians 5:23
[a]Rom 15:33
[b]1 Thess 3:11
[c]Luke 1:46f; Heb 4:12
[d]James 1:4; 2 Pet 3:14
[e]1 Thess 2:19

1Thessalonians 5:24
[a]1 Cor 1:9; 2 Thess 3:3
[b]1 Thess 2:12

1Thessalonians 5:25
[1]Two early mss add *also*
[a]Eph 6:19; 2 Thess 3:1; Heb 13:18

1Thessalonians 5:26
*a*Rom 16:16

1Thessalonians 5:27
*a*Col 4:16
*b*Acts 1:15

1Thessalonians 5:28
*a*Rom 16:20; 2 Thess 3:18

Koine Greek

1Th. 5:1 Περι δε των χρονων και των καιρων, αδελφοι, ου χρειαν εχετε υμιν γραφεσθαι. [2] Αυτοι γαρ ακριβως οιδατε οτι η ημερα κυριου ως κλεπτης εν νυκτι ουτως ερχεται· [3] οταν γαρ λεγωσιν, Ειρηνη και ασφαλεια, τοτε αιφνιδιος αυτοις εφισταται ολεθρος, ωσπερ η ωδιν τη εν γαστρι εχουση, και ου μη εκφυγωσιν. [4] Υμεις δε, αδελφοι, ουκ εστε εν σκοτει, ινα η ημερα υμας ως κλεπτης καταλαβη· [5] παντες υμεις υιοι φωτος εστε και υιοι ημερας· ουκ εσμεν νυκτος ουδε σκοτους· [6] αρα ουν μη καθευδωμεν ως και οι λοιποι, αλλα γρηγορωμεν και νηφωμεν. [7] Οι γαρ καθευδοντες νυκτος καθευδουσιν· και οι μεθυσκομενοι, νυκτος μεθυουσιν. [8] Ημεις δε, ημερας οντες, νηφωμεν, ενδυσαμενοι θωρακα πιστεως και αγαπης, και περικεφαλαιαν, ελπιδα σωτηριας. [9] Οτι ουκ εθετο ημας ο θεος εις οργην, αλλ' εις περιποιησιν σωτηριας δια του κυριου ημων Ιησου χριστου, [10] του αποθανοντος υπερ ημων, ινα, ειτε γρηγορωμεν ειτε καθευδωμεν, αμα συν αυτω ζησωμεν. [11] Διο παρακαλειτε αλληλους, και οικοδομειτε εις τον ενα, καθως και ποιειτε.

1Th. 5:12 Ερωτωμεν δε υμας, αδελφοι, ειδεναι τους κοπιωντας εν υμιν, και προισταμενους υμων εν κυριω, και νουθετουντας υμας, [13] και ηγεισθαι αυτους υπερ εκπερισσου εν αγαπη δια το εργον αυτων. Ειρηνευετε εν εαυτοις. [14] Παρακαλουμεν δε υμας, αδελφοι, νουθετειτε τους ατακτους, παραμυθεισθε τους ολιγοψυχους, αντεχεσθε των ασθενων, μακροθυμειτε προς παντας. [15] Ορατε μη τις κακον αντι κακου τινι αποδω· αλλα παντοτε το αγαθον διωκετε και εις αλληλους και εις παντας. [16] Παντοτε χαιρετε· [17] αδιαλειπτως προσευχεσθε· [18] εν παντι ευχαριστειτε· τουτο γαρ θελημα θεου εν χριστω Ιησου εις υμας. [19] Το πνευμα μη σβεννυτε· [20] προφητειας μη εξουθενειτε· [21] παντα δε δοκιμαζετε· το καλον κατεχετε· [22] απο παντος ειδους πονηρου απεχεσθε.

1Th. 5:23 Αυτος δε ο θεος της ειρηνης αγιασαι υμας ολοτελεις· και ολοκληρον υμων το πνευμα και η ψυχη και το σωμα αμεμπτως εν τη παρουσια του κυριου ημων Ιησου χριστου τηρηθειη. [24] Πιστος ο καλων υμας, ος και ποιησει.

1Th. 5:25 Αδελφοι, προσευχεσθε περι ημων.

1Th. 5:26 Ασπασασθε τους αδελφους παντας εν φιληματι αγιω. [27] Ορκιζω υμας τον κυριον, αναγνωσθηναι την επιστολην πασιν τοις αγιοις αδελφοις.

1Th. 5:28 Η χαρις του κυριου ημων Ιησου χριστου μεθ' υμων. Αμην.

Process of Discovery

Linguistics Section

Linguistic Structure

1. 9 For God hath not appointed us to wrath, but to the acquisition of life, by our Lord Jesus the Messiah:

    Another example of the makeup of the congregation.

2. [18] And in every thing be thankful: For this is the pleasure of God in Jesus the Messiah, concerning you

    This verse continues to demonstrate that the congregation was converted Jews.

3. [23] And may the God of peace sanctify you all, perfectly, and keep blameless your whole spirit, and your soul, and your body, till the coming of our Lord Jesus the Messiah.

    Another example of the congregation being mainly Jews.

4. [28] The grace of our Lord Jesus the Messiah be with you. Amen.

    The final verse of the letter continues to demonstrate the makeup of the congregation.

The NASB 1995 was used for the chiastic structure.

[The second coming of Yeshua] 1Th. 5:1   Now as to the [a]times and the epochs, brethren, you [b]have no need of anything to be written to you. [2] For you yourselves know full well that [a]the day of the Lord [1]will come [b]just like a thief in the night. [3] While they are saying, "[a]Peace and safety!" then [1b]destruction [2]will come upon them suddenly like [1]labor pains upon a woman with child, and they will not escape. [4] But you, brethren, are not in [a]darkness, that the day would overtake you [1b]like a thief; [5] for you are all [a]sons of light and sons of day. We are not of night nor of [b]darkness; [6] so then let us not [a]sleep as [1b]others do, but let us be alert and [2c]sober. [7] For those who sleep do their sleeping at night, and those who get drunk get [a]drunk at night. [8] But since [a]we are of *the* day, let us [b]be [1]sober, having put on the [c]breastplate of [d]faith and love, and as a [e]helmet, the [f]hope of salvation. [9] For God has not destined us for [a]wrath, but for [b]obtaining salvation through our Lord Jesus Christ, [10] [a]who died for us, so that whether we are awake or asleep, we will live together with Him. [11] Therefore [a]encourage one another and [b]build up one another, just as you also are doing.

[Final Exhortations] 1Th. 5:12 But we request of you, brethren, that you [1a]appreciate those [b]who diligently labor among you, and [c]have charge over you in the Lord and give you [2]instruction, [13] and that you esteem them very highly in love because of their work. [a]Live in peace with one another. [14] We urge you, brethren, admonish [a]the [1]unruly, encourage [b]the fainthearted, help [c]the weak, be [d]patient with everyone. [15] See that [a]no one repays another with evil for evil, but always [b]seek after that which is good for one another and for all people. [16] [a]Rejoice always; [17] [a]pray without ceasing; [18] in everything [a]give thanks; for this is God's will for you in Christ Jesus. [19] [a]Do not quench the Spirit; [20] do not despise [a]prophetic [1]utterances. [21] But [a]examine everything *carefully;* [b]hold fast to that which is good; [22] abstain from every [1]form of evil.

1Th. 5:23 Now [a]may the God of peace [b]Himself sanctify you entirely; and may your [c]spirit and soul and body be preserved complete, [d]without blame at [e]the coming of our Lord Jesus Christ. [24] [a]Faithful is He who [b]calls you, and He also will bring it to pass.

1Th. 5:25 Brethren, [a]pray for us[1].

1Th. 5:26 [a]Greet all the brethren with a holy kiss. [27] I adjure you by the Lord to [a]have this letter read to all the [b]brethren.

1Th. 5:28 [a]The grace of our Lord Jesus Christ be with you.

Discussion

This final chapter is broken into two messages. The first message is about the second coming of Yeshua. The final part of the letter contain some exhortations.

Questioning the narrative

1. What are the children of light versus darkness? (v. 5)

    Light is symbolic of goodness and godliness, while darkness is symbolic of evil and Satan. To be a Yeshua follower, one needs to be filled with goodness and godliness.

2. What is the breastplate of faith and love? (v. 8)

    Paul was speaking metaphorically. The breastplate of faith and love is the spiritual knowledge of having faith that life with Yeshua will bring about righteousness and entry into the Kingdom of Heaven. Faith and love will get a person through the rough spots of life.

3. What is the helmet of hope and life? (v. 8)

    Paul is speaking metaphorically. The congregation was told to keep their hope in their worship of Yeshua and to follow his way. Following the ways of Yeshua leads to a good life in accordance with the LORD's wishes and the hope of eternal life with Yeshua in Heaven.

Culture Section

Discussion

In Paul's day, many of the desert tribes raided one another to plunder in the middle of the night. In many parts of the Near East, plundering and taking spoils were considered lawful. The stealing of sheep and goats was common. The shepherds would sleep with the flocks, but if the thief was quiet, the animals at the edges of the flock could be easily taken. This stealing occurred at night because even if the shepherd was awake it is hard to see in the dark. Paul likened Yeshua's return to the thief in that no one knew exactly when it was going to happen.

Paul warned the congregation that false prophets would come into their presence. As noted earlier there were other expressions of Christianity during Paul's time. The rumor of Yeshua's quick return started in Macedonia. These converts did not have any Scriptures. They believed in the Messiah but had little knowledge of Yeshua's ways. The signs of his return was famine and war which was happening in Macedonia. The people became weary and prayed for Yeshua's return. This event would have stopped the wars and famine. Yeshua was thought to take care of his followers. The end of the world idea came from the false messiahs mentioned in Matthew's Gospel.[15]

Kissing in the Near East in Paul's day was done on the cheek. Semitic people would kiss each other during festivals, weddings, religious services and to greet each other on the streets. Kissing was a sign of sincerity, true affection, and a bond of peaceful relations. A holy kiss implies that the kiss is done with the love of Yeshua.

Questioning the passage

1. What does verse seven mean?

   Near Easterners did not drink strong drinks and high alcohol content wine duing the day. During the day Semitic people were sober. In the evenings they

---

[15] Rocco A. Errico and George M. Lamsa, *Aramaic Light on Galatians through Hebrews: A Commentary Based on Aramaic, the Language of Jesus, and Ancient near Eastern Customs* (Smyma, GA: Noohra Foundation, 2005).

drank wine in their homes. An exception to this rule was at wedding celebrations. All the guests would drink excessively and became drunk. Therefore, some people slept at night while other persons got drunk at night.[16]

2. What does the term "spirit" mean in verse twenty-three?

   In this verse the word spirit means God's breath. This is the essence of God in every person which helps them distinguish between right and wrong. In Aramaic the word *ruha* can mean "spirit, prophecy, pride, wind, and rheumatism."[17]

Thoughts

The second coming of Yeshua was important to the early congregations of Jews who turned to Yeshua. They were under persecution, famine and caught in the middle of wars that occurred between different groups in the Roman Empire. Following Yeshua was supposed to bring love and peace. But it did not. Becoming a follower of Yeshua did not open the doors to a good life. Why should the people in Thessalonia stay dedicated to Yeshua? Paul tells them it is the second coming of Yeshua that they needed to be aware of. When would this happen? No one knew when this would happen. Paul leaves the congregation with the instructions to keep on the course and things will improve.

---

[16] IBID.

[17] IBID.

Bibliography

Errico, Rocco A., and George M. Lamsa. *Aramaic Light on Galatians through Hebrews: A Commentary Based on Aramaic, the Language of Jesus, and Ancient near Eastern Customs*. Smyma, GA: Noohra Foundation, 2005.

"Home." AwesomeStories, June 17, 2020. https://awesomestories.org/.

"Home." Bible Study. Accessed July 20, 2022. https://www.biblestudy.org/bible-study-by-topic/people-in-the-bible/timothy.html.

Murai, Hajime. "Literary Structure (Chiasm, Chiasmus) of First Epistle to the Thessalonians." Literary structure (chiasm, chiasmus) of each pericopes of First Epistle to the Thessalonians. Accessed July 20, 2022. http://www.bible.literarystructure.info/bible/52_1Thessalonians_pericope_e.html.

"Paul in the Bible - His Life and Story." biblestudytools.com. Accessed July 20, 2022. https://www.biblestudytools.com/topical-verses/paul-in-the-bible/.

Read, 2 minute. "Who Is Silvanus in the Bible? ." BibleAsk, June 3, 2022. https://bibleask.org/who-is-silvanus-in-the-bible/.